DALLAS
MAVERICKS

by Ray Frager

Published by ABDO Publishing Company, 8000 West 78th Street, Edina, Minnesota 55439. Copyright © 2012 by Abdo Consulting Group, Inc. International copyrights reserved in all countries. No part of this book may be reproduced in any form without written permission from the publisher. SportsZone™ is a trademark and logo of ABDO Publishing Company.

Printed in the United States of America,
North Mankato, Minnesota
062011
092011

 THIS BOOK CONTAINS AT LEAST 10% RECYCLED MATERIALS.

Editor: J Chris Roselius
Copy Editor: Anna Comstock
Series design and cover production: Christa Schneider
Interior production: Carol Castro

Photo Credits: Sue Ogrocki/AP Images, cover; Eric Gay/AP Images, 1; David J. Phillip/AP Images, 4, 37, 43 (middle); LM Otero/AP Images, 7, 28; Tom DiPace/AP Images, 9, 43 (bottom); Mark Elias/AP Images, 10, 42 (middle); AP Images, 13, 23; Susan Ragan/AP Images, 14; Reed Saxon/AP Images, 16, 42 (top); Suzy Mast/AP Images, 19; Mark Terrell/AP Images, 20; Tim Johnson/AP Images, 24; Pat Sullivan/AP Images, 27; Tony Dejak/AP Images, 31; Kent Horner/AP Images, 32; Kevin Frayer/AP Images, 34, 43 (top); Greg Wahl-Stephens/AP Images, 38; Mark Humphrey/AP Images, 41, 42 (bottom); Tony Gutierrez/AP Images, 44, 47

Library of Congress Cataloging-in-Publication Data
Frager, Ray.
 Dallas Mavericks / by Ray Frager.
    p. cm. -- (Inside the NBA)
 Includes index.
 ISBN 978-1-61783-154-6
 1. Dallas Mavericks (Basketball team)--History--Juvenile literature. I. Title.
 GV885.52.D34F73 2012
 796.323'64'097642812--dc23
                          2011021709

TABLE OF CONTENTS

Chapter 1 ....Champions at Last, 4

Chapter 2 ....Early Struggles, 10

Chapter 3 ....Finding Success, 16

Chapter 4 ....Turning It Around, 24

Chapter 5 ....A Model Franchise, 34

Timeline, 42

Quick Stats, 44

Quotes and Anecdotes, 45

Glossary, 46

For More Information, 47

Index, 48

About the Author, 48

CHAMPIONS AT LAST

The Dallas Mavericks had been among the top teams in the National Basketball Association (NBA) for years. But they always seemed to fall just short when it mattered most.

The Mavs entered the 2010–11 season with 10 straight 50-win seasons. Despite that regular-season success, the club had reached the NBA Finals just one time. In 2006, they had lost to the Miami Heat in the NBA Finals. They made the playoffs in each of the next four seasons after that but were eliminated in the first or second round every time.

Star forward Dirk Nowitzki received most of the blame for Dallas's failures. Critics said the 2007 NBA Most Valuable Player (MVP) did not have what it took to lead his team to a title.

However, the 2010–11 Mavericks had a different look from the previous teams that had fallen just short. Only Nowitzki and guard Jason Terry

The Mavs' Dirk Nowitzki (41) goes for a shot against the Miami Heat's Joel Anthony (50) during Game 4 of the 2011 NBA Finals.

THE KIDD

While suiting up for Team USA, Jason Kidd had a perfect 58–0 record. That included gold medals at the 2000 and 2008 Olympic Games. Although he had firmly established himself as one of the best point guards of his generation, Kidd was not so lucky with his NBA teams. That is, until 2011.

The Mavericks took Kidd with the second pick in the 1994 draft. They traded him to the Phoenix Suns in 1996. He then played more than 10 seasons with the Suns and later the New Jersey Nets. Kidd led the Nets to back-to-back NBA Finals in 2002 and 2003, but lost both times. The Nets then traded him back to the Mavericks in 2008.

Following his 2011 title, Kidd was second in the NBA in career assists and third in steals and three-pointers made. The 10-time All-Star was an almost certain future Hall of Famer.

remained from the 2006 team. The team had surrounded those players with proven veterans such as point guard Jason Kidd, forward Shawn Marion, and center Tyson Chandler. They combined with young point guard J. J. Barea to give the Mavs a formidable core.

After finishing 57–25 and earning the third seed in the Western Conference, Dallas again appeared vulnerable during the 2011 playoffs. The Portland Trail Blazers took two of the first four games of their first-round series.

Then the Mavs got hot. Dallas won the next two games. The Mavs swept the defending champion Los Angeles Lakers in the second round. After defeating the upstart Oklahoma City Thunder in the conference finals, the Mavericks met the Heat

Mavericks guard Jason Terry tries to get around the Heat's Juwan Howard during Game 3 of the 2011 NBA Finals.

in a rematch of the 2006 NBA Finals.

Despite the Mavs' play-off success and veteran roster, many analysts still picked the Heat to win. Miami had dominated past playoffs. And the Heat featured three superstars—LeBron James, Dwyane Wade, and Chris Bosh.

Few were surprised when Miami took a 2–1 series lead. Even the Mavericks' win in Game 2 was close. Dallas trailed by 15 points in the middle of the fourth quarter. But Nowitzki scored the final nine points for Dallas, including a layup with three seconds remaining, to hand the Mavs a 95–93 victory.

However, Nowitzki had torn a tendon in a finger on his non-shooting hand during Game 1. He was battling a 101-degree temperature due to a sinus infection going into Game 4. As before, Nowitzki and the Mavs looked like they were going to fall just short of winning the big one. But then the momentum shifted.

Despite his illness, Nowitzki led Dallas with 21 points and 11 rebounds to an 86–83 win in Game 4. Then he scored 29 points and grabbed six rebounds in a 112–103 win in Game 5. The teams headed back to Miami. Dallas just needed to win one of a possible two games there to take the NBA title.

The Mavericks' players made it clear they wanted the series to end in six games. But that seemed unlikely after Nowitzki made only one of his 12 shots and scored only three points during the first half.

Still, Dallas held a 53–51 lead at the half. And then Nowitzki heated up. He made eight of his 15 shots in the second half. He ended with 21 points, including 10 in the final eight minutes of the game. Terry added 27 points coming off the bench.

The only two players remaining from the 2006 Mavericks squad led the team to a 105–95 win in Game 6—and the franchise's first NBA championship.

The Mavs and head coach Rick Carlisle celebrate their first-ever NBA title after taking Game 6 105–95 to win the Finals series against the Heat.

"Dirk and Jet [Terry] have had to live for five years with what happened in 2006," Dallas coach Rick Carlisle said. "As of tonight, those demons are officially destroyed."

For the series, Nowitzki averaged 26 points and 9.7 rebounds per game. The versatile 7-foot power forward was unanimously named the Finals MVP. With plenty of help from his veteran team-mates, Nowitzki had led the Mavs to their first NBA title. They had come a long way from their humble expansion-team beginnings in 1980.

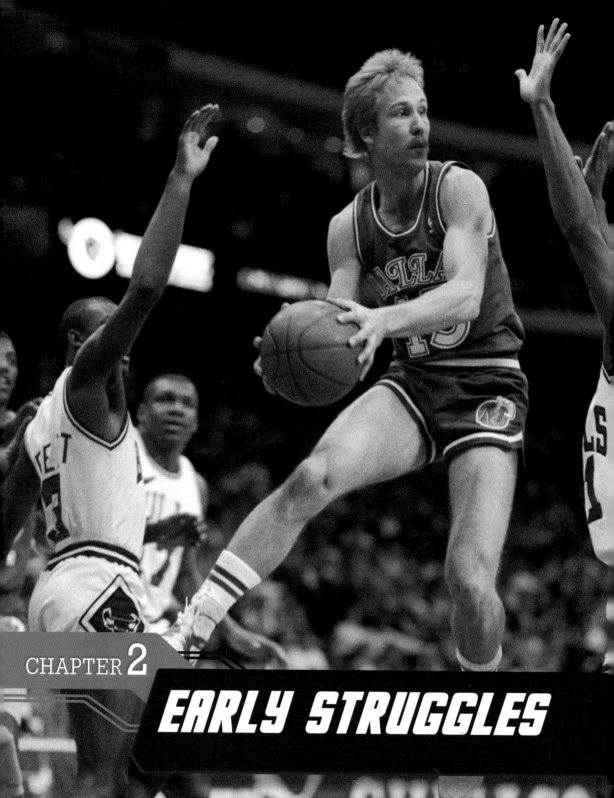

EARLY STRUGGLES

CHICAGO

For six years, the Chaparrals of the American Basketball Association (ABA) had played in Dallas. But they moved south to San Antonio in 1973 and became the Spurs. In 1980, pro basketball finally returned to North Texas. That was when the NBA awarded an expansion team to Dallas.

Wanting to get people excited about the new team, the club held a contest inviting fans to submit nicknames. The winner was Mavericks. Some people believe the name came from the television show *Maverick*, which ran from 1957 to 1962. There was also an ABA team that had played in Houston from 1967 to 1969 called the Mavericks. The ABA was a second professional league that merged with the NBA in 1976.

The newly named Dallas Mavericks hired Dick Motta to become their first head coach. Two years before, Motta had

Dallas guard Brad Davis, *center*, was a fan favorite and played with the Mavericks from 1980 to 1992.

DALLAS'S ABA TEAM

The first professional basketball team in Dallas, the Chaparrals of the ABA, played there from 1967 to 1973. In an attempt to increase fan numbers, the team changed its name to the Texas Chaparrals in 1970–71. The Chaps then played games in three different cities in Texas: Dallas, Fort Worth, and Lubbock. But the name change did not last long. The next season the team went back to being called the Dallas Chaparrals and played all home games in Dallas.

The Chaparrals were successful on the court. They made the playoffs in five of their six seasons. But they still struggled to draw fans to the games. In their last game in Dallas, the Chaparrals drew fewer than 150 paying fans. After the season, Red McCombs, John Schaefer, and other investors bought the team. They then moved it to San Antonio before the start of the 1973–74 season.

led the Washington Bullets to an NBA championship. The Mavericks' home would be the new Reunion Arena, which had just opened in April 1980.

The early years were rough for Dallas, which is typical for new teams. The Mavericks' first NBA Draft pick was Kiki Vandeweghe of the University of California, Los Angeles. But Vandeweghe did not want to join a team that was likely to lose a lot of games. So the Mavericks traded the unhappy forward to the Denver Nuggets one month into their inaugural 1980–81 season. They received two future first-round draft picks in exchange.

Featuring a roster of young players, Dallas went 15–67 in its first season. Only three of the team's 21 players had more than three seasons of professional experience.

Mavericks forward/guard Mark Aguirre, *left*, drives around Rodney McCray, *right*, of Houston in a 1988 playoff game.

Geoff Huston was the Mavericks' leading scorer. He averaged 16.1 points per game before being traded in the middle of the season. The top scorer remaining at the end of the season was Jim Spanarkel, who averaged 14.4 points per game. Tom LaGarde averaged 8.1 rebounds per game to lead the team. Guard Brad Davis, who joined the team early in the season, was another bright spot for the Mavs. He averaged 6.9 assists per game. That would have ranked in the NBA's top 10 if he had played enough games to qualify.

After that rough first year, the Mavericks looked forward to their two picks in the first round of the 1981 NBA Draft. They

Mavericks guard Rolando Blackman, *left*, dribbles around Gerald
Wilkins of the New York Knicks in 1990.

used them wisely, selecting
forward/guard Mark Aguirre
and guard Rolando Blackman.
With one of their two second-
round picks, they took forward
Jay Vincent. All three players
became productive members
of the team and helped lift the
Mavs to respectability.

After a slow start in
1981–82, the Mavs finished
the season with 28 wins—13
more than the previous season.
Aguirre, who averaged 18.7

points per game, missed 31 games with an injury. Vincent, however, stepped up and became the team's leading scorer with 21.4 points per game. Blackman added 13.3 points per game, and Davis contributed another 12.1 points per game.

The Mavericks continued to improve the next season. They won 38 games. Owning a 25–24 record at the All-Star break, the Mavericks were competing for a postseason spot. But a seven-game losing streak late in the season left them out of the playoffs.

The Mavericks credited their improvement to strong fundamentals. Dallas's average of 16.4 turnovers per game was the lowest in the league. Aguirre, Vincent, and Blackman continued to provide solid play, as well. Aguirre averaged 24.4 points per game to rank

sixth in the league. Vincent averaged 18.7 points per game, and Blackman averaged 17.7 points per game. In addition, Davis ranked 10th in the NBA in assists with 7.2 per game.

With a solid base of young players, the Mavericks were ready to become a team the rest of the NBA would have to pay attention to.

CHAPTER 3

FINDING SUCCESS

I n the 1983–84 season, the Dallas Mavericks left behind the expansion-team tag. Thanks to several good draft picks, the team's sharp eye for talent started to show. Dallas entered a five-year stretch in which they made the playoffs and had a winning record each season.

In its first playoff season, 1983–84, Dallas finished 43–39. Forward Mark Aguirre emerged as a true star. In fact, he became the first Mavericks player to compete in the NBA All-Star Game. Aguirre finished second in the league in scoring, with 29.5 points per game. Guard Rolando Blackman also ranked among the NBA's top 20 scorers, with 22.4 points per game.

The Mavericks won their first-ever playoff series in thrilling fashion. Facing the Seattle

Mark Aguirre (24) goes in for two points while Kareem Abdul-Jabbar, *right*, of the Los Angeles Lakers defends during a 1988 playoff game.

THE LONGEST SECOND

The Dallas Mavericks won their first playoff series in 1984. In the clinching game, the deciding play came in the final second—twice. The Mavericks held onto a slim one-point lead with one second left in overtime. Dallas attempted to end the game by throwing the ball off of Tom Chambers, one of the players from the Seattle SuperSonics. Chambers instead caught the ball and launched a long shot that missed as time expired. The Mavericks celebrated the victory, and the SuperSonics headed to the locker room. However, the referees ruled that the clock had not started. So, 14 minutes after they thought the game was over, the teams returned to the court to play that final second. The Sonics, who had been given possession, tried a lob pass to Chambers that he was not able to catch. For the second time in the last second, the Mavs won the game.

SuperSonics in a best-of-five format, Dallas won the series by claiming a 105–104 overtime victory in Game 5. The game had to be played in Southern Methodist University's Moody Coliseum in Dallas, which could only hold approximately 9,000 fans. That was because Reunion Arena was occupied by a tennis tournament. The Mavericks then faced the Los Angeles Lakers in the second round, and Dallas was eliminated four games to one.

Despite coming off a good season, the Mavericks owned the fourth pick in the 1984 NBA Draft. They had acquired it in an earlier trade. Dallas selected forward/center Sam Perkins from North Carolina. The Chicago Bulls had selected third. They drafted Perkins' former teammate—future Hall of Famer Michael Jordan.

Dallas forward Sam Perkins (44) shoots over Mark Alarie, *right*, of the Washington Bullets during a game in 1989.

With the addition of Perkins in 1984–85, the Mavericks improved by one game to finish with a 44–38 record. This time, however, Dallas did not get past the first round of the playoffs. They lost to the Portland Trail Blazers.

Aguirre had another good season. He scored 25.7 points per game. His teammates

Embarrassing Moment

In Game 4 of the 1984 playoff series against the Los Angeles Lakers, rookie guard Derek Harper lost track of the score. Thinking the Mavericks were ahead by one point even though the game was actually tied, Harper dribbled the ball as the final seconds of regulation time disappeared. He instead should have tried to get a shot to win the game. The Lakers eventually won in overtime.

James Donaldson, *right*, is guarded by Kareem Abdul-Jabbar, *left*, of the Lakers in a 1988 playoff game.

Blackman and Jay Vincent gave the Mavs three consistent scorers. Blackman averaged 19.7 points per game, and Vincent added 18.2. The Mavericks also led the league in three-point baskets. Brad Davis led the team with 47, while second-year forward/guard Dale Ellis added 42.

Aguirre the Scorer

The Mavericks could almost always count on Mark Aguirre to get 20 points or more in every game. Though he was not the biggest of NBA players at 6 feet 6 inches, Aguirre could get a lot of his points close to the basket with post-up moves. He also was able to hit outside shots. Defensive players had to respect both parts of his game, making him difficult to guard.

Dallas again finished 44–38 the following season, in 1985–86. During that season, the club made a significant move by trading for veteran James Donaldson. The 7-foot-2, 275-pound center was brought in to stabilize a position the Mavericks had previously used several starters to fill.

Donaldson did not score a lot of points, averaging close to 10 points per game during his seven years in Dallas. But he was a reliable rebounder. He averaged close to 10 rebounds and between one and two blocked shots per game.

The Mavericks did not need Donaldson to score. Aguirre averaged 22.6 points per game, and Blackman averaged 21.5 points per game that season. Perkins, Vincent, and Derek Harper, who took over for Davis as a starting guard, averaged between 12 and 15 points per game for the Mavericks.

The Mavs got past the Utah Jazz in the first round of the 1986 playoffs, but they again lost in the second round. This time, the Lakers eliminated Dallas in six games.

The Mavericks had their best season up to that point by winning 55 games in 1986–87. The team also won the Midwest Division title for the first time. The Mavs had a lot of talented players and a strong starting unit. Two young and talented players, Detlef Schrempf and

Roy Tarpley, provided punch off the bench. Schrempf was a 6-foot-9 forward in his second season, and Tarpley was a 6-foot-11 rookie center/forward.

The Mavericks started the 1987 postseason with a bang. Taking on the Seattle Super-Sonics, Dallas scored a club-record 151 points in Game 1 to cruise to an easy win. But the Mavericks then lost the next three games and were eliminated. After the season, Dick Motta resigned as coach and was replaced by John MacLeod.

Under MacLeod, the Mavericks had another strong season in 1987–88, going 53–29. Tarpley was outstanding in his second year in the NBA. He averaged 13.5 points and 11.8 rebounds per game. His rebound average ranked seventh in the league. Tarpley also won the NBA Sixth Man Award, which is

given to the player who is voted the best substitute in the league.

In the playoffs, the Mavs had their best showing yet. Dallas defeated the Houston Rockets in the first round and took down the Denver Nuggets in the second round. They then faced the Lakers for the Western Conference championship and a spot in the NBA Finals. The Lakers earned home-court advantage, which proved to be the difference in the series. The Mavericks won each of their three home games, but they lost the deciding Game 7 in Los Angeles.

Derek Harper, *right*, became the starting point guard for Dallas during the 1985–86 season. Harper played 12 seasons for the Mavericks.

Still, the Mavericks had reason to feel optimistic about their future. They had a core of young, talented players who proved they could produce during the regular season, as well as perform in the pressure of the playoffs. But things were about to change for the worse.

CHAPTER 4

TURNING IT AROUND

The Mavericks believed they were close to winning a title after coming within one game of the NBA Finals in the 1987–88 season. Instead, they actually were about to start a long downward slide. Starting in 1990–91, Dallas missed the postseason for 10 straight years and finished each of those seasons with a losing record.

Dallas started well in 1988–89, winning nine of their first 12 games. But injuries and roster changes resulted in a 38–44 record. The Mavs lost Roy Tarpley in January when the NBA suspended him because of a drug problem. In February, Dallas traded Mark Aguirre, the team's first star player, to the Detroit Pistons for Adrian Dantley. The Mavericks also traded Detlef Schrempf to the Indiana Pacers for center/forward Herb Williams. The Mavs then lost center James

Roy Tarpley catches a pass during a 1988 playoff game against the Houston Rockets. Tarpley was suspended and finally banned from the NBA due to substance abuse problems during his career.

ALWAYS TO BE REMEMBERED

As of 2011, only two players have had their numbers retired by the Dallas Mavericks: Brad Davis (15) and Rolando Blackman (22). Davis played for the Mavs from 1980 to 1992 and was always a fan favorite. Signed as a free agent in December 1980, Davis became the first Maverick to have his jersey retired. He shares the club record with Michael Finley for most consecutive three-pointers made with 10, and he led Dallas in assists during the team's first six seasons.

Blackman was a first-round draft pick by the Mavericks in 1981. He played 11 seasons for Dallas before finishing his career with the New York Knicks. As a member of the Mavs, Blackman was named to the NBA All-Star Team four times. His 16,643 points and 6,487 field goals were team records at the time of his retirement from the NBA in 1994.

Donaldson to injury in March, forcing him to miss about 30 games of the season. Due to the many distractions, it was not surprising the Mavericks missed the 1989 playoffs.

The next season featured even more drama. Richie Adubato replaced head coach John MacLeod, who was fired after only 11 games. Tarpley returned from his drug suspension. When on the court, Tarpley averaged 16.8 points and 13.1 rebounds per game for the 45 games he played. However, he was suspended once again after being arrested on charges of driving while intoxicated in November 1989. He missed nearly half the season.

The Mavericks somehow managed to post a winning record for 1989–90. They went 47–35 and qualified for the playoffs. Dallas's stay in the playoffs was brief, though.

Dallas's Jim Jackson (24) drives toward the basket while being guarded by the Heat's Brian Shaw, *right*, in 1993.

The Portland Trail Blazers eliminated the Mavs in three straight games in the first round.

That 1990 playoff appearance would be the Mavericks' last one for a while. The 1990–91 team sank to a 28–54 record. The Mavs had added veteran forward Alex English. During his prime, he averaged 20 to 25 points per game. But by the time he got to Dallas, English was 36 years old and no longer the player he had once been. In his last season in the NBA, English averaged just 9.7 points per game. Tarpley was injured early in the season and played only five games. In March,

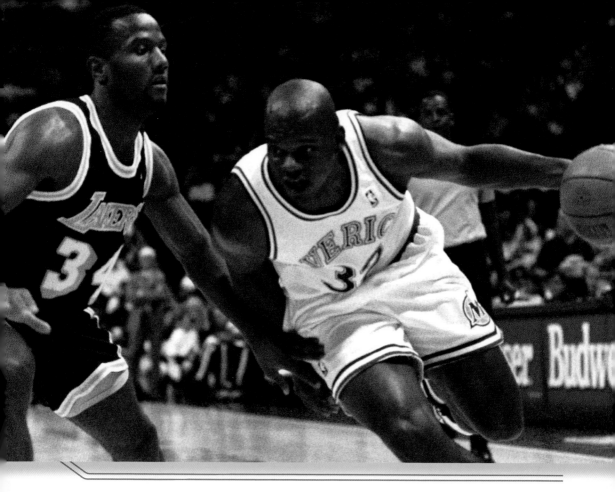

The Mavs' Jamal Mashburn, *right*, heads to the basket while being guarded by George Lynch, *left*, of the Lakers in 1995.

Tarpley was arrested for a second time on a DWI charge and hit with another suspension.

The Mavs went 22–60 in 1991–92 and suffered a 15-game losing streak. Rolando Blackman had another fine season, averaging 18.3 points per game. But it would be his last in a Dallas uniform. After the season, the Mavericks traded their all-time leading scorer to the New York Knicks for a first-round draft pick.

Dallas's 1992–93 season started on a bad note when first-round draft pick Jim Jackson refused to sign a contract with the Mavericks for several months. As a result of his hold-out, he played only 28 games for Dallas. The Mavs ended that season 11–71. At the time, that was the second worst record in NBA history.

The following season, 1993–94, Jackson was with the team from the start. The Mavericks also added forward Jamal Mashburn through the draft. But the losing continued for the Mavs. Dallas was 3–40 at the end of January. The team played a little better in the closing months, but still finished just 13–69.

Coach Quinn Buckner was fired after the season. The Mavericks hired back Dick Motta, their original coach. With the second overall selection in the draft, they picked point guard Jason Kidd. The pick was just what the team needed. With Kidd, Jackson, and Mashburn,

Hall of Fame Mavericks

There are three former Mavericks players who are now members of the Naismith Memorial Basketball Hall of Fame: Alex English, Adrian Dantley, and Dennis Rodman. English played for Dallas in 1990–91, while Dantley wore a Mavs uniform from 1989 to 1990. Rodman appeared in 12 games for the Mavericks in 2000.

the Mavericks had hopes of once again becoming a winning team. The Mavericks started to turn things around in 1994–95. They went 36–46 that season.

That year, Kidd shared the NBA's Rookie of the Year Award with the Detroit Pistons' Grant Hill. Kidd recorded four triple-doubles to lead the league. A triple-double is when a player has double-digit figures in three statistical categories. For the season, Kidd averaged 11.7 points and 7.7 assists per game. That ranked him 10th in the NBA. He also grabbed 5.4 rebounds per game, which is a high total for a guard.

Jackson, now in his third season, and Mashburn, in his second year, were the Mavericks' top scorers. Jackson averaged 25.7 points per game, and Mashburn averaged 24.1 points per game. Allowed back into the NBA after his drug suspension, Tarpley averaged 12.6 points and 8.2 rebounds per game in 55 games.

The positive turnaround did not continue. The Mavericks won 10 fewer games the next season, going 26–56. Individually, Kidd improved on his rookie numbers. He averaged 16.6 points, 9.7 assists, and 6.8 rebounds per game. His assists average was second in the league. But Mashburn had to have knee surgery after 18 games. Tarpley was banned again from the NBA because he

An All-Time Great

Don Nelson started his coaching career at age 36 in 1976 and did not stop coaching until after the 2009–10 season. He started coaching in 1976 with the Milwaukee Bucks and stayed there until taking over the Golden State Warriors in 1988–89. He also coached the New York Knicks, Dallas Mavericks, and then Golden State again, where he finished his career. Nelson retired as the NBA's all-time wins leader.

did not follow the terms of his treatment for substance abuse. He did not play for Dallas that season or ever again in the NBA.

After the 1995–96 season, coach Dick Motta was fired. Owner Donald Carter, who had worked so hard to bring the Mavericks to Dallas, then sold the team. The buyers were a group led by Ross Perot Jr., whose father had run for president in 1992.

In 1996–97, Dallas finished with almost the same

Michael Finley flies toward the basket for two points in 1997. The Mavericks acquired Finley from Phoenix in 1996.

record as the season before, 24–58. But the changes that had started after the previous season continued. The Mavericks surprisingly traded Kidd, Jackson, and Mashburn during the season.

Kidd was traded first. He was sent to the Phoenix Suns in December along with two other players for forward/center A. C. Green, point guard Sam Cassell, and guard/forward Michael Finley.

Mavericks center Shawn Bradley, *left*, blocks a shot by Utah Jazz center Greg Ostertag in 2001.

In February, shortly after Don Nelson became general manager, Mashburn was traded to the Miami Heat for three players. Later that month came another huge trade involving nine players. Jackson, Cassell, and three other Mavericks went to the New Jersey Nets. Coming to Dallas was Shawn Bradley, a 7-foot-6 center, and three other players. Bradley finished the season as the NBA's leader in blocked shots with 3.4 per game.

Despite the many changes, Dallas continued to struggle the next two seasons. The Mavericks won just 20 games in 1997–98 and finished 19–31 in the strike-shortened 1998–99 season. Still, Finley averaged more than 20 points per game in each season.

Finally, in 1999–2000, the Mavs showed signs of new life. They did not make the playoffs, but they improved to 40–42. They finished the season by winning nine of their last 10 games.

Dirk Nowitzki, a second-year player for Dallas, gave fans a glimmer of hope. The 7-foot forward from Germany began to emerge as an NBA star. He averaged 17.5 points per game. That was approximately nine more than in his

A Familiar Owner

When Mark Cuban bought the Dallas Mavericks in 2000, he was hardly a stranger to many members of the team. That is because Cuban had been a season ticket holder for several years. During home games, Cuban could be seen in his courtside seat. And seldom was he quiet. The outspoken Cuban was often yelling at referees or talking to players. With Cuban as the owner, the franchise has become one of the best in the league. It consistently wins 50 or more games every season.

rookie season. Nowitzki ranked among the league's best three-point shooters, finishing second in the three-point contest at the NBA All-Star Game.

In 2000, the team was sold to Mark Cuban. With Cuban in charge, the Mavericks would finally become a success again.

CHAPTER 5

A MODEL FRANCHISE

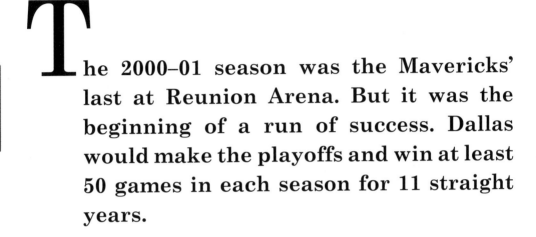

T he 2000–01 season was the Mavericks' last at Reunion Arena. But it was the beginning of a run of success. Dallas would make the playoffs and win at least 50 games in each season for 11 straight years.

The Mavs went 53–29 in 2000–01. A trio of stars emerged to lead the way. Dirk Nowitzki averaged 21.8 points and 9.2 rebounds per game. Michael Finley averaged 21.5 points, 5.2 rebounds, and 4.4 assists. In his third season with Dallas, Steve Nash became the starting point guard and averaged 15.6 points and 7.3 assists per game.

The Mavs solidified their lineup with an eight-player trade with the Washington Wizards during the season. Forward Juwan Howard was

Guard Steve Nash, *right*, makes a pass as Toronto forward Jerome Williams, *left*, looks on in 2002. Nash played for the Mavericks from 1998 to 2004.

the most important player that Dallas acquired in the trade. In 27 games with the Mavs, he averaged 17.8 points and 7.1 rebounds per game.

In the playoffs for the first time since 1989–90, the Mavericks lost their first two games against the Utah Jazz. But Dallas rallied to win the last three games and advance to the second round. However, the San Antonio Spurs eliminated the Mavs in the next round.

The Mavericks moved to American Airlines Center in 2001–02. Dallas set a team record for victories with 57.

Again, the Mavericks made a multiple-player trade during the middle of the season. One year after acquiring Howard, the Mavs sent him to the Denver Nuggets. In return, Dallas received guard Nick Van Exel, among others.

In the 2002 playoffs, Dallas swept the Minnesota Timberwolves in three games in the opening round. The Sacramento Kings, however, defeated Dallas four games to one in the second round.

The Mavericks reached 60 victories for the first time in 2002–03, finishing 60–22. They generated so much excitement in Dallas that all of the team's home games were sold out for the first time. Nowitzki, Finley, and Nash each turned in another outstanding season. Off the bench, Van Exel contributed 12.5 points and 4.3 assists per game.

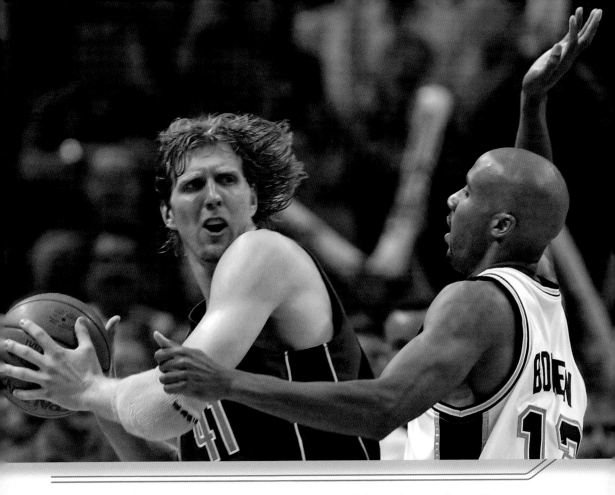

Mavs forward Dirk Nowitzki, *left*, keeps the ball from Spurs player Bruce Bowen, *right*, during a playoff game in 2006.

In the playoffs, the Mavs survived two seven-game series in the first and second rounds to face the rival San Antonio Spurs in the Western Conference finals. The Spurs once again eliminated the Mavericks in six games. The next two seasons, the Mavericks dropped off a bit. They went 52–30 in 2003–04, and 58–24 in 2004–05. They lost in the first and second rounds of the playoffs during those years, respectively.

Dallas lost a star player before 2004–05 when point guard Steve Nash signed with the Phoenix Suns as a free

Mavericks guard Jason Terry, *left*, tries to get around Portland's Gerald Wallace, *right*, in 2011.

agent. Jason Terry took over Nash's starting role.

Even without Nash, Dallas finished the season 58–24. Nowitzki led the team in scoring with 26.1 points. In March, coach Don Nelson resigned. Avery Johnson was named the interim coach and finished the season with a 16–2 record. The Mavericks beat the Houston Rockets in the first round of the playoffs. But the Suns, led by Nash, defeated Dallas in the second round.

In his first full season as coach, Johnson guided the Mavericks to a 60–22 record, the second best in the Western Conference. They again had to get past the Spurs in the playoffs, this time in a second-round series. It was a tight, back-and-forth series. The Mavs finally advanced with an overtime victory in Game 7. Then Dallas defeated the Suns in six games in the conference finals. That sent the Mavericks to the NBA Finals for the first time in team history.

Dwyane Wade and the Miami Heat awaited. However, playing in front of their home crowd in Dallas, the Mavs won the first two games. When the series shifted to Miami, Dallas appeared to be headed for a 3–0 series advantage when it

built a 13-point lead in Game 3. But the Heat roared back and claimed a 98–96 victory. The Mavericks did not win another game in the series.

It was a disappointing ending. But with Nowitzki, Terry, swingman Jerry Stackhouse, and young forward Josh Howard back in 2006–07, the Mavs looked poised to make another run. They appeared on their way as Nowitzki averaged 24.6 points per game en route to being named the league's MVP. Dallas finished the season 67–15 and the top seed in

WRONG CALL

In Game 5 of the 2006 NBA Finals, the Dallas Mavericks had a chance to pull out a victory. But a mistake by their power forward Josh Howard proved costly. With 1.9 seconds left in overtime, Dwyane Wade of the Miami Heat made the first of his two free-throw attempts. Howard then called for a timeout. Mavs coach Avery Johnson had wanted to save the timeout until Wade shot his second free-throw attempt, allowing Dallas to inbound the ball at half-court. But it was too late. Wade made his second free throw to give Miami a one-point lead. The Mavs then had to inbound the ball from under their own basket, and they missed a rushed shot, losing the game in the process. Johnson said the officials should have let him take back the timeout that Howard called. But the referees disagreed. The head referee, Joe Crawford, said, "Not only once, but twice [Howard] asks for a timeout. [I was] forced to call it, simple as that."

the Western Conference. But in the first round of the play-offs, the eighth-seed Golden State Warriors shocked Dallas with a six-game series victory. Nowitzki struggled in the final game of the series, shooting just 2-for-13 from the field.

The Mavericks continued to win at least 50 games over the next three seasons, but they lost in the first round of the playoffs two times. The team made several key personnel moves during that time. During the 2007–08 season, All-Star point guard Jason Kidd returned to Dallas in a trade with the New Jersey Nets. Rick Carlisle was hired as the team's coach after that season. In 2009, they traded Stackhouse in a four-team deal that resulted in Shawn Marion joining the Mavs. Then, before the 2010–11 season, the Mavs traded for Tyson Chandler.

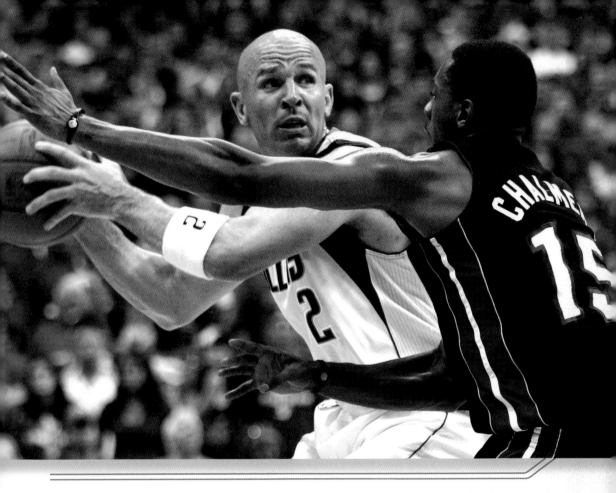

Veteran Dallas guard Jason Kidd, *left*, protects the ball from the Heat's Mario Chalmers, *right*, in Game 5 of the 2011 NBA Finals.

The 2010–11 season started with everyone looking at the Los Angeles Lakers, the Miami Heat, or the Boston Celtics to win the NBA title. But with its veteran roster, Dallas won 57 games. After a slow start against the Portland Trail Blazers, the Mavs rolled all the way to a rematch with the Heat and their first NBA title.

With their first championship behind them and the leadership of Nowitzki, Terry, and Kidd, the Mavericks gave fans hope that another championship would not be too far off.

TIMELINE

1973 The ABA's Chaparrals play their last game in Dallas on March 26.

1980 The NBA's new Dallas Mavericks play their first game on October 11 and beat the San Antonio Spurs 103–92.

1983 On January 14, Mark Aguirre records the first triple-double in team history with 30 points, 11 rebounds, and 16 assists in a victory over the Denver Nuggets.

1984 On April 26, the Mavericks defeat the Seattle SuperSonics 105–104 in overtime to win their first playoff series.

1987 Dallas wins more than 50 games in a season for the first time, finishing 55–27. The Seattle SuperSonics stun the Mavericks in the first round of the playoffs, winning the series in four games.

1989 The Mavericks trade Aguirre on February 15 to the Detroit Pistons for Adrian Dantley and a first-round draft choice.

1992 The Mavericks trade Rolando Blackman to the New York Knicks on June 24 for a first-round draft choice.

1994 The Mavericks take point guard Jason Kidd with the second pick in the NBA draft. He is reacquired by the team in 2008.

1997	On February 17, the Mavericks and the New Jersey Nets complete a nine-player trade that includes sending Jim Jackson to New Jersey.
2001	The Mavericks play their first game at the American Airlines Center on October 30.
2001	Dallas ends a streak of 10 consecutive losing seasons by finishing the year with a 53–29 record.
2004	On July 14, Dallas loses Steve Nash when he signs with the Phoenix Suns as a free agent.
2006	The Mavericks compete in the NBA Finals for the first time in team history. Dallas loses 4–2 to the Miami Heat.
2007	Dallas forward Dirk Nowitzki is named the MVP after averaging 24.6 points, 8.9 rebounds, and 3.4 assists per game during the regular season.
2007	Dallas finishes the regular season with a league-best 67–15 record, but they have a very short playoff run. The Golden State Warriors upset the Mavericks in the first round of the postseason, winning the series four games to two.
2008	On March 8, Nowitzki passes Blackman to become the all-time leading scorer in team history.
2011	Dallas finishes the season with 57 wins, marking the 11th straight year the Mavericks win at least 50 games. They go on to defeat the Miami Heat in the Finals, winning the franchise's first NBA title.

QUICK STATS

FRANCHISE HISTORY

Dallas Mavericks (1980–)

NBA FINALS
(1980– ; win in bold)

2006, **2011**

CONFERENCE FINALS

1988, 2003, 2006, 2011

DIVISION TITLES

1987, 2007, 2010

KEY PLAYERS
(position[s]; years with team)

Mark Aguirre (F; 1981–89)
Rolando Blackman (G; 1981–92)
Erick Dampier (C; 2004–10)
Brad Davis (G; 1980–92)
James Donaldson (C; 1985–92)
Michael Finley (G/F; 1996–2005)
Derek Harper (G; 1983–94; 1996–97)
Jim Jackson (G; 1992–97)
Jason Kidd (G; 1994–96; 2008–)
Jamal Mashburn (F; 1993–97)
Steve Nash (G; 1999–2004)
Dirk Nowitzki (F; 1998–)
Sam Perkins (F/C; 1984–90)
Roy Tarpley (F/C; 1986–90; 1994–95)
Jay Vincent (F; 1981–86)

KEY COACHES

Avery Johnson (2005–08):
    194–70; 23–24 (postseason)
Dick Motta (1980–87; 1994–96):
    329–409; 11–17 (postseason)
Don Nelson (1997–2005):
    339–251; 19–24 (postseason)

HOME ARENAS

Reunion Arena (1980–2001)
American Airlines Center (2001–)

* All statistics through 2010–11 season

QUOTES AND ANECDOTES

Before he signed with the Mavericks in their first season, Brad Davis was playing in the minor-league Continental Basketball Association for a team in Anchorage, Alaska.

In the 2002–03 season, the Mavericks set an NBA record for fewest turnovers per game, averaging just 11.6.

Mavericks forward A. C. Green was known for rarely missing a game. In November 1997, he set an NBA record by playing in his 907th consecutive game.

In January 2002, Mavericks owner Mark Cuban criticized the NBA's head of referees, Ed Rush, saying he "wouldn't hire him to manage a Dairy Queen." Because people from Dairy Queen thought he was belittling them, Cuban worked part of a day at one of their stores. "They challenged me to come and manage a Dairy Queen, saying it wasn't that easy," Cuban said. "And so I got up at 6 a.m., learned how to make a Blizzard, learned how to make a dip cone, and I still never got the dip thing right."

"Well, obviously it's a great honor to be the all-time leading scorer for this franchise. There have been so many great players along the way. Ro Blackman is a friend of mine, and he coached the German National team one year so I'm really, really close to him, so I hate to break that record and take it from him, but it's definitely a great honor for me." —Dirk Nowitzki on becoming the team's all-time leading scorer in 2008, surpassing Rolando Blackman

GLOSSARY

assist

A pass that leads directly to a made basket.

contract

A binding agreement about, for example, years of commitment by a basketball player in exchange for a given salary.

draft

A system used by professional sports leagues to select new players in order to spread incoming talent among all teams. The NBA Draft is held each June.

expansion

In sports, the addition of a franchise or franchises to a league.

franchise

An entire sports organization, including the players, coaches, and staff.

free agent

A player whose contract has expired and who is able to sign with a team of his choice.

general manager

The executive who is in charge of the team's overall operation. He or she hires and fires coaches, drafts players, and signs free agents.

interim

Temporarily holding a position until a permanent replacement is found.

postseason

The games in which the best teams play after the regular-season schedule has been completed.

rebound

To secure the basketball after a missed shot.

rival

An opponent that brings out great emotion in a team, its fans, and its players.

rookie

A first-year player in the NBA.

FOR MORE INFORMATION

Further Reading

Ballard, Chris. *The Art of a Beautiful Game: The Thinking Fan's Tour of the NBA*. New York: Simon & Schuster, 2009.

Hubbard, Jan (editor). *The Official NBA Encyclopedia*. New York: Doubleday, 2000.

Simmons, Bill. *The Book of Basketball: The NBA According to the Sports Guy*. New York: Ballantine/ESPN Books, 2009.

Web Links

To learn more about the Dallas Mavericks, visit ABDO Publishing Company online at **www.abdopublishing.com**. Web sites about the Mavericks are featured on our Book Links page. These links are routinely monitored and updated to provide the most current information available.

Places to Visit

American Airlines Center
2500 Victory Avenue
Dallas, TX 75219
214-222-3687
www.americanairlinescenter.com
This has been the Mavericks' home arena since 2001. The team plays 41 regular-season games here each year. Tours are available when the Mavericks are not playing.

Naismith Memorial Basketball Hall of Fame
1000 West Columbus Avenue
Springfield, MA 01105
413-781-6500
www.hoophall.com
This hall of fame and museum highlights the greatest players and moments in the history of basketball. Alex English and Adrian Dantley are among the former Mavericks enshrined here.

Texas Sports Hall of Fame
1108 South University Parks Drive
Waco, TX 76706
252-256-1600
www.tshof.org
This hall of fame and museum celebrates and preserves Texas sports history. Mavericks guard Rolando Blackman was inducted here in 2008.

INDEX

Adubato, Richie (coach), 26
Aguirre, Mark, 14–15, 17, 19, 21, 25
American Airlines Center, 36

Barea, J. J., 6
Blackman, Rolando, 14–15, 17, 20–21, 22, 26, 28
Bradley, Shawn, 32–33
Buckner, Quinn (coach), 29

Carlisle, Rick (coach), 9, 40
Carter, Donald (owner), 30
Cassell, Michael, 31–32
Chandler, Tyson, 6, 40
Cuban, Mark (owner), 33, 36

Dantley, Adrian, 25, 29
Davis, Brad, 13, 15, 20–21, 26
Donaldson, James, 21, 25–26

Ellis, Dale, 20
English, Alex, 27, 29

Finley, Michael, 26, 31, 33, 35–36

Green, A. C., 31

Harper, Derek, 19, 21
Howard, Josh, 39, 40
Howard, Juwan, 35–36
Huston, Geoff, 13

Jackson, Jim, 28–32
Johnson, Avery (coach), 38–39, 40

Kidd, Jason, 6, 29–31, 40–41

LaGarde, Tom, 13

MacLeod, John (coach), 22, 26
Marion, Shawn, 6, 40
Mashburn, Jamal, 29–32
Motta, Dick (coach), 11, 15, 22, 29–30

Nash, Steve, 35–39
NBA Finals
    2006, 5, 7, 39, 40
    2011, 6–9, 41
Nelson, Don (coach and general manager), 30, 32, 38–39
Nowitzki, Dirk, 5, 7–9, 33, 35–36, 38–40

Perkins, Sam, 18–19, 21
Perot, Ross, Jr. (owner), 30

Reunion Arena, 12, 18, 35
Rodman, Dennis, 29

Schrempf, Detlef, 21–22, 25
Spanarkel, Jim, 13
Stackhouse, Jerry, 39–40

Tarpley, Roy, 22, 25–28, 30
Terry, Jason, 5, 8–9, 38–39, 41

Van Exel, Nick, 36, 39
Vandeweghe, Kiki, 12
Vincent, Jay, 14–15, 20–21

Williams, Herb, 25

About the Author

Ray Frager is a freelance writer based in the Baltimore, Maryland, area. He has been a professional sports editor and writer since 1980. He has worked for the *Trenton Times*, the *Dallas Morning News*, the *Baltimore Sun*, FOXSports.com, and Comcast SportsNet. At the *Sun*, he edited books on Cal Ripken Jr., the building of Baltimore's football stadium, and the Baltimore Ravens' 2000 Super Bowl season. Frager has also written books on the Baltimore Orioles and Pittsburgh Pirates.